D1720664

the human dimension

the human dimension

SWEDISH INDUSTRIAL DESIGN

EDIZIONI BOLIS

The Human Dimension is
the result of a collaboration between the Swedish Technical Attaché System,
the Swedish Work Environment Fund and the Swedish Industrial Design Foundation.
Thanks are due to everyone who supported the project,
in particular the Swedish Work Environment Fund and the Swedish Institute
for having made this publication possible.

© 1994 SVENSK INDUSTRIDESIGN

EDITED BY TORSTEN DAHLIN, DANIELE MASCANZONI, GUSTAF ROSELL OCH LISBETH SVENGREN.
PRODUCTION BY LARS GRÖNKVIST.
TRANSLATION FROM SWEDISH TO ENGLISH BY FRANCES VAN SANT AND CATHERINE STUART.
TRANSLATION FROM ITALIAN TO ENGLISH BY FIONA JOHNSTON.
GRAPHIC DESIGN BY BIRGITTA ADOLFSSON.
COVER PHOTO BY GEORG SESSLER.
PHOTOS PAGE 10, 18–19, 23, 28–29, 45, 59, 67, 79, 80–81, 85, 92–93 BY GEORG SESSLER,
PAGE 14–15, 32–33, 74–75 BY PETER DE RY, PAGE 58 STEWEN QUIGLEY, PAGE 61 JANN LIPKA.
ALL OTHER PHOTOS COURTESY OF THE COMPANIES.
PRINTED IN ITALY BY POLIGRAFICHE BOLIS, BERGAMO, 1994.

ISBN 91 630 2884 0

THE EXHIBITION
THE HUMAN DIMENSION HAS BEEN DESIGNED BY ALFONSO GRASSI & ASSOCIATI,
GRAPHIC PROJECT BY EDUARD W. HARTUNG DE HARTUNGEN AND SOUND PROJECT BY AUDIO DESIGN.

CONTENTS

preface

BY
DANIELE MASCANZONI

For some of you, this book may be a discovery, for some others it may stir up the past, and for others again it may be a confirmation. However, one factor will be common – that it will not be difficult for you to agree, at least ideologically, with the values of The Human Dimension and recognize the necessity to re-evaluate the concept of design for Man, distant from the estheticism we have become accustomed to in recent times, an interesting subject in its own right, but one which lacks content.

If any human values deserve to be restored, one is certainly solidarity towards others. One way of putting this into practice would be to manufacture products everyone can use, irrespective of age, state of health or degree of disability. In the present day, numerous articles – far too many – have reached an unacceptable level of complexity for the user. The degree of technological sophistication has become a part of the marketing strategy, but can also produce serious practical frustration. The products lack maturity and the functional content the user really needs. In particular, there is a shortage of mediation as a means of intelligent communication with the consumer.

Tackling product development within a whole project is a question of industrial culture and maturity, yet it is a problem which must be faced simply because the product should be adapted to the consumer and not vice-versa. Intelligent use of technology (as a means, not an end) may help to simplify this procedure, and the values behind The Human Dimension may become the premises for a great project of the future, a project where "human" and esthetic values are fused to create objects which are perfectly harmonious in shape and function.

Current consumer awareness also contributes to the trend of purchasing something on the basis of the article's real usefulness, with greater attention paid to the content. This is particularly true for some market areas which are growing in importance: the elderly, for example, are increasingly "young" and active and their needs have changed; and the disabled, who quite rightly refuse to have passive roles in society. For some time now, they have been demanding equal opportunities and they are tired of being mortified by insensitive, if not downright mindless, design. The designer's role is therefore fundamental in the development of products based on the careful analysis of the user's needs and his environment. From here, there will be a progression to an interdisciplinary design model in continual symbiosis with this concept.

The criteria of The Human Dimension are the starting points for the creation of well-designed products for the human species seen in its entirety. Differences are therefore taken into consideration with no vacuous definitions of "normality." In addition, objects created specifically for one limited group may also be extremely useful for others.

Moreover, in some cases, the most useful objects originate in other sectors. Take mountaineering equipment and clothing, for example. These were developed for the professionals, but have evolved to include the production of high-performance gear which is comfortable and practical for everyone. This becomes even more evident in the work environment, where ergonomic studies are behind the development of safe, rational, professional equipment, which also leads to the development of high-quality tools destined to a wider public. And as we all know, quality is no longer an optional, but a basic ingredient for the survival of any company.

Creation of products suitable for everyone, irrespective of age, sex or physical ability, is also a question of respect for human dignity. In a society with a truly human dimension, the man-machine interface must be such that first and foremost, it will not damage the user's health, but will respect diversities in the same way that correct town-planning eliminates the structural barriers.

So it is not just a question of esthetics and function alone, but also one of content, with a shift in attitude from formalism to something substantial. When the historians look back, they do not analyze wars, governments or scientific discoveries alone – they also take a close look at the "fringe" events and the utensils that were in everyday use at the time. In the future, when we look back over this period, we will also see the everyday items, and the things belonging to The Human Dimension, are designed and built to be remembered.

Milan, october 1994

NEXT PAGE:
A MODEL CHAIR TAKES SHAPE UNDER THE HANDS OF CABINETMAKER ÅKE AXELSSON.
HIS FURNITURE FOR HOMES AND OFFICES HAS HAD A SOLID REPUTATION FOR MANY YEARS.

dynamic
design

BY
TORSTEN DAHLIN

this book is a complement to the exhibition Swedish Industrial Design – The Human Dimension. The exhibition is addressed to an interested general public, to shed light on how design is expressed in Swedish products. In contrast to the traditional, static way of exhibiting and judging products taken out of their context, here the dynamic qualities of the products are exhibited. Only when a product is used is it possible to understand what is specifically Swedish design.

11

Industrial design is an integral part of industrial development. Swedish industry is particularly export-oriented and is dominated by over 20 transnational corporations that manufacture industrial goods and consumer capital goods. Most smaller Swedish companies are suppliers that produce commodities, or companies that manufacture tools and aids.

Companies producing consumer goods, particularly for the living environment, are the most important bearers of the concept of Scandinavian design. As this industrial sector becomes less significant, what is meant by Swedish design is also changing.

Two main lines

Industrial design in Sweden has been developed along two main lines. One follows the European, international line towards more advanced form. The form and shape are of primary importance.

The second line is more focused on needs and the user. The form or shape is thus subordinate to or integrated into the technology and function, and reflects a functionalistic approach.

Industrial products are always the result of a process in which the product is designed and manufactured. This process is in turn a prerequisite for other subsequent processes. The quality of the first process determines to a large extent how the product will be accepted and used in the next stage.

This book will show how these two dynamic processes can be linked to The

Human Dimension and how they can be united in the product and its usage. The possibility of affecting the design of a product generally depends on how technologically advanced it is. Simple products for the home and leisure, for example, are more design-intensive. A product's design is in itself a strong factor aiding its competitiveness. Products used in our working lives and in production systems, on the other hand, are more technology-intensive. The design is guided by technology and function and the designer must often subordinate him/herself to goals such as better quality and accessibility.

New possibilities

In contrast to this is the rapid development in electronics. This development has provided new possibilities for completely new products, and has provided a basis for methods of development and design directly linked to production. To describe the dynamic relationships between the product and how it is used in different processes, we have chosen four themes that are typical areas of focus for Swedish industrial design: *Care and Caring, More Beautiful Everyday Things, The Good Job and Recreation.*

Care and Caring is the area in which Swedish industrial design is currently receiving a large amount of international attention. Ergonomics in the widest sense of the word has been developed furthest here, and applied to assist the elderly, the sick, and people with impaired mobility, sight and hearing. These efforts have been the models for the development of methods that focus on the user´s needs and requirements.

More Beautiful Everyday Things is the best known area of Swedish design efforts. Things used in our everyday lives are not just traditional utility goods, but also products that have been adapted to different age groups and environments.

The Good Job describes investments in research about and changes in the work environment. These efforts have now placed Sweden in the international vanguard for integrating occupational health work, research results and industrial design work in production in which the human being is the focus. The choice of products and the design of the work-place have been determined by the requirements of both the tasks done there and the worker.

Recreation shows products from small companies where the drive and enthusiasm of individual entrepreneurs have resulted in products of high quality. Most of the products and applications shown are original and unique for the Scandinavian countries, e.g., long-distance ice skating and Telemark skiing.

It is an understanding of design´s potential to communicate that we want to demonstrate. Design is not just the esthetic expression of products: industrial design is also a profession and a tool for co-operation across areas of competence; to create understanding for the user´s needs and demands during the process in which products are created. It is hoped that this exhibition and book will open up a dialog between foreign and Swedish experts in separate design disciplines on a more comprehensive approach to form, function and design.

NEXT PAGE: ERICSSON'S NEW GH 337 FOR THE GSM NETWORK IS A POCKET TELEPHONE WORTHY OF THE NAME. AT ONLY 193 GRAMS, IT IS THE WORLD'S LIGHTEST GSM TELEPHONE. THE FORM OF THE GH 337 IS THE WORK OF RICHARD LINDAHL.

THE HUMAN DIMENSION

BY
GUSTAF ROSELL

Swedish products are a little bit different. The design process is motivated by ideals different from those that are usually associated with design elsewhere in the world. The best Swedish products reflect ideals such as functionality, democracy and simplicity. The simple and functional can of course be pretty dull. The ideal Swedish simplicity is instead refined, elegant and perhaps even sublime. The functional aspect in Swedish products is not that of classical functionalism, but the function experienced by the user – regardless of what the technical solution looks like. We who worked on this exhibition have called this The Human Dimension.

It is actually a development that has been under way for quite a long time, but has simply not been given a name until now. In the 1990s several different trends with common characteristics have met to form a whole.

The original humanists were a free association of educated Italians who re-discovered the culture of classical times as the middle ages were coming to a close. Humanism has also given rise to more general ideals that can be summarized as a respect for humanity and a desire for knowledge. The knowledge aspired to was broad and universal, the Italian *uomo universale*, rather than one-sided and specialized. A further aspect of humanism is the value it places on benefit to humanity, one interpretation of which can be that technological progress should have as its expressed goal the betterment of the universal human condition.

The humanism that is the basis for this exhibition is closer to the original Italian humanism than to later philosophical trends such as new humanism and Marxist humanism. There are several things about Swedish design and Swedish product development methods that accord with the ideals of the original humanists.

A bit of history

Modernism had a great influence on Swedish designers and industrial designers. Functionalism was the main theme of the Stockholm Exhibition, which was held in 1930. Swedes have always spoken of functionalism rather than modernism, although they are stylistically quite similar. A magazine, *Acceptera*, was published in connection with the exhibition, and became quite influential. It promoted new, absolute ideals of beauty and faith in the future in the functionalist spirit. On the political scene, the concept of *folkhem*, or the People's Home – as Swedes still describe their welfare state – had been formulated by the Social Democratic prime minister Per Albin Hansson a few years earlier.

These events began the spread of an attitude, and actually even a working method, which in a kind of democratic spirit aspired to make beautiful, good quality, affordable goods available to laborers as well as salaried employees. Naturally, there were many political overtones in the ideology that was being formed. The good ideas from that time are now found in most political camps and are strongly anchored in Swedish culture and industrial tradition.

Sweden did not participate in the second

NEXT PAGE:
A HOSPITAL ORDERLY LIFTS ABOUT 320 KILOS PER WORK DAY. ARJO HAS BEEN IMPROVING HOSPITAL EQUIPMENT FOR 30 YEARS, OFTEN WORKING IN COLLABORATION WITH THE USERS.

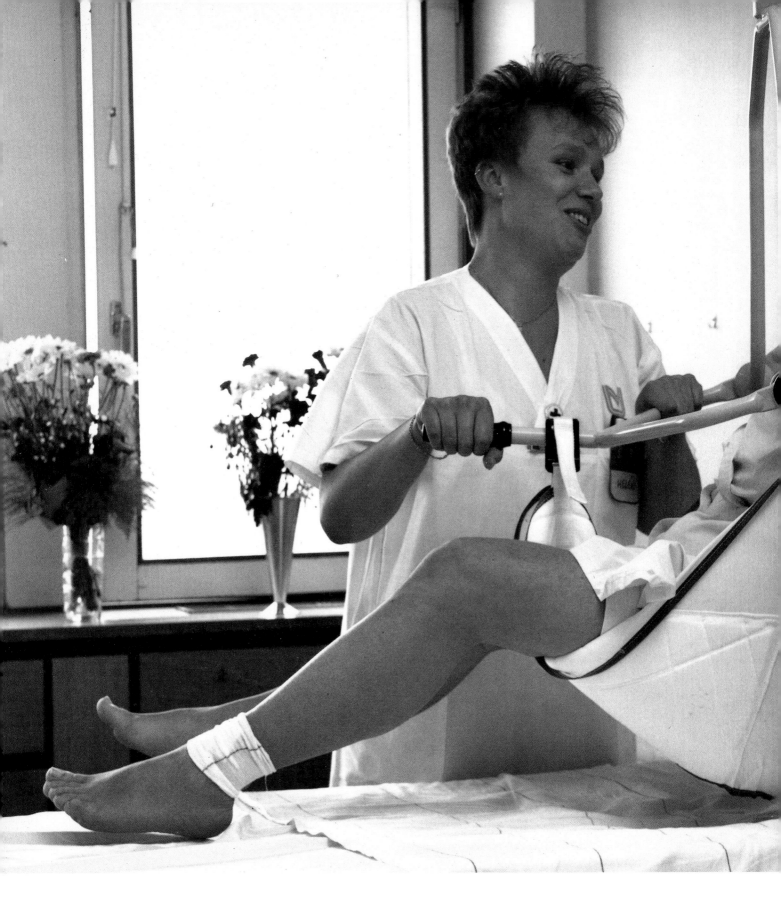

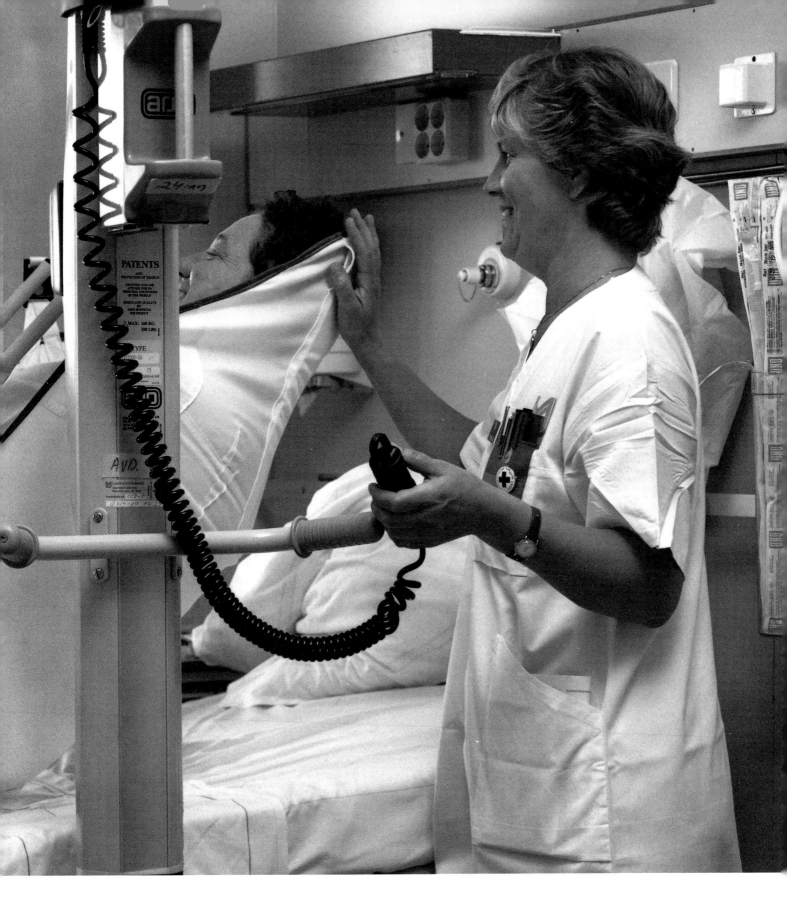

World War. The war put a stop to the development of functionalism in other countries. In Sweden, it lived on until the 1950s. Some might even argue that it lived on until the 1970s.

It was during the 1950s that Swedish design had its era of greatness, particularly in the furniture industry, when a light, airy style was developed with strong roots in functionalism. A further important epoch was the intensive research in the 1970s on the work environment, ergonomics and equipment for people with disabilities. Esthetics, and particularly superficial "styling" were then regarded almost as bad words, which made contact with industry somewhat rough at times and the epoch in general rather poor in visually effective design.

These historical events form the background for The Human Dimension. In the 1990s the balance between the various components and historical influences is more harmonious than perhaps ever before.

From its original emphasis on the work environment and products that are handled, the user-oriented approach has become increasingly important for technically complex systems. The explanation is simple. We have reached a kind of technological pain threshold with regard to our ability to manage and understand our increasingly complicated technology. Technological refinements that can not meet a specific user need are losing their power as sales arguments and becoming disadvantages instead.

Ideals and ideologies

The most important ideal for Swedish products in the humanistic tradition is consideration and respect for the user. This corresponds to the original humanist's respect for humanity. During the entire design process, the focus is on the user. Representative users are often included in the design groups, and thus have a concrete effect on the design of the products. The requirements of the users are particularly important when it is not the user that makes the purchase decision, which is frequently the case with products used in industry, hospitals or offices. The user-centered working method is even more important when the users can not choose their own products.

User-oriented design can be regarded as a special form of market adaptation. The relationship with marketing is an important part of a product's success. Ergonomics and user-friendliness are therefore frequently given considerable emphasis when products are marketed.

The ideology of The Human Dimension also includes constantly improving our knowledge of ergonomics and use. This corresponds to the humanist´s desire for knowledge. Specialists in ergonomics are often called in on development projects, and research frequently proceeds parallel with the actual development work. In many cases the Swedish Work Environment Fund has been able to finance those parts of the project that are of general interest. A design process of this nature is clearly a group endeavor, and this is another of the most important basics in the Swedish design tradition. The group should preferably consist of several different experts that form a multidisciplinary team. In our technologically complex society it is no longer possible for one person to know about everything, like the universal geniuses of the Renaissance *uomo universale,* did. Today it is the knowledge of the group that counts.

Ideals like teamwork and consideration for the user distinguish the Swedish design tradition from those of other countries, as well as from other creative disciplines in Sweden where the designer expresses himself and his own ideals and creativity in the form of the products. The group-oriented design process, however, does not allow particular individuals to express their egos. This is perhaps why it is not particularly glamorous to be an industrial designer in Sweden. It is the pride of the group and the common origin of its ideas that are the most important motivating factors.

Who is normal?

Many of the previous exhibits of Swedish design have been in the area of aids for people with disabilities. Visitors occasionally ask, only half in jest, if Sweden has an unusually large number of disabled people. We haven't, of course, but after 25 years of research and development we do have a large number of products.

The basic principle is that as many products and environments as possible should be made accessible for all. People with disabilities need some special equipment in order to live ordinary lives. It is one of their rights as citizens to have access to such equipment.

This view frequently does not lead to products that are specially adapted for people with disabilities, but rather to improvement of ordinary products so that they can also be used by people with some degree of functional impairment such as arthritis.

The products are then often better for non-impaired people as well. This is not actually a matter of design for people with disabilities, but design for a wider range of users: "design for a broader average."

Interest in this type of design is currently increasing. One reason is clear to see: it is the progressive ageing of the European population. There have been several activities on the theme of design for elderly people, and more are planned. This group has been traditionally regarded as having little buying power, but this is changing. Not only are older people becoming more numerous, they also seem to be staying more active longer. As consumers, they are among the most hard to please. They will not accept products that are designed primarily to look good in advertisements with smiling young models.

Not extravagant

The identifying characteristic of the esthetics of The Human Dimension is that is not extravagant. Some typical qualities are simplicity, lightness, restrained elegance, a pronounced feeling for materials, light colors and attention to details. The simplicity of The Human Dimension is warm, not clinically sterile. There are few decorations. The functional components are used in the functionalist spirit, as the main decorations and primary elements of the form.

This spareness can be traced to the strong functionalist currents at the beginning of the century. Other important reasons are Sweden's severe climate and history. Sweden was a poor country for a long time, and could not afford excesses. A clear historical example is the Swedish modification of the flowing rococo style, which became an extremely restrained style with few, but exquisite, decorative touches.

Swedish products usually have sculptured forms. One reason is that in the design process building models is often at least as important as drawing. The three-dimensional qualities of the form are more important than the two-dimensional ones.

Instead of working with patterns, the inherent qualities of the material predominate. Natural materials such as birch, linen and rubber are important, but a sensitive treatment of synthetic materials is also a clear characteristic.

Since the turn of the century, there has been a Swedish tradition of mechanical innovation. There is thus something kin to the Italian fascination with *la bella macchina*. The esthetics of the machine has also left its mark on Swedish design. It is not unusual for the technical functions themselves to be emphasized as esthetic elements.

The criteria of The Human Dimension are dynamic rather than static. It is the dynamics of a product, its qualities in use, that is important – not how it looks in a glass case.

The way it might be

An underlying theme in all parts of The Human Dimension is a desire to make technological progress relevant and useful. The ideals of The Human Dimension can be combined with respect for the environment to become important driving forces behind developments in both technology and the market economy.

OPPOSITE PAGE: EVERY YEAR, ABOUT 300,000 PATIENTS AROUND THE WORLD GET A PACEMAKER FROM SIEMENS-ELEMA. THE OPERATION TAKES 30 TO 90 MINUTES. PER-ERIK JARL HAS DESIGNED THIS PACEMAKER, WHICH WON A PRIZE FOR EXCELLENT SWEDISH DESIGN IN THE SPRING OF 1994.

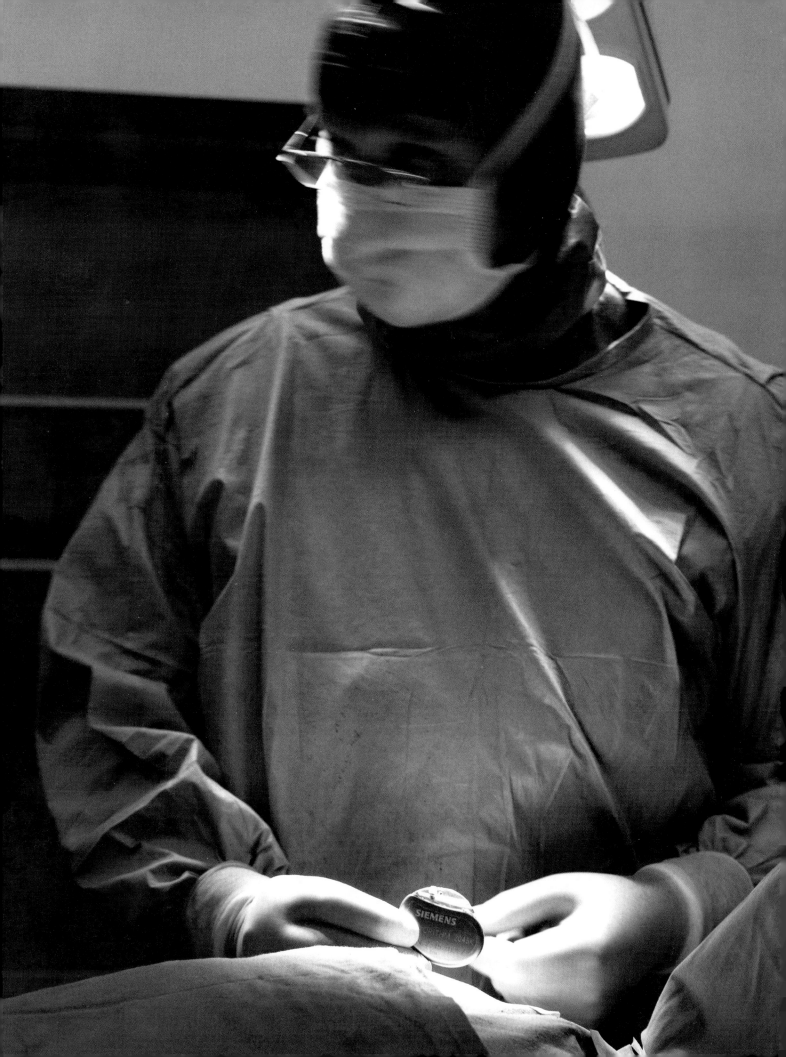

HUMAN ENGINEERING SHOWED THE WAY

BY
KERSTIN WICKMAN

In America, the first generation of industrial designers had often begun as commercial artists, scenographers or fashion designers. In Italy, industrial designers almost without exception had started as architects. In Sweden, many of the first industrial designers had been trained as engineers, or – as in Sixten Sason's case – were artists with a passion for technology. These diverse backgrounds still influence attitudes and approaches in these countries.

It was the engineers who, in the years around the turn of the century, established the foundations for the large Swedish industries: ASEA, Atlas Copco, Electrolux, AGA, Bahco, Ericsson.

A friend

Different cultures and individuals have different mechanisms for integrating changes and innovations. However, for most of this century, Swedes in general have been full of enthusiasm for all the new technologies – machines powered by electricity, new farm equipment, efficient mass production. Technology was not an enemy but a friend.

Some historians of technology have claimed that the Swedish trust in technology and desire to make work more efficient were born in two gigantic construction projects of the last century: the Göta canal and the Hjälmare canal, both completed in the 1830s. As the laborers toiled and dug, their work functioned as a school in technology.

A further reason for the high status of engineers early in this century was the introduction and development of electricity. In Sweden, with its many rivers and abundant water power, the production and distribution of electrical power was a challenge calling for the art of the engineer.

New industries

The Federation of Swedish Industries, *Industriförbundet*, was founded in 1910 by

Sigfrid Edström, who had been the head of ASEA, Allmänna Svenska Elektriska AB, since 1903. ASEA can be regarded as a counterpart to AEG in Germany. Just as AEG was to pioneer a new kind of industrial architecture and design, ASEA cultivated its image as a company of the future. Under Edström's leadership many aspects of production were streamlined, and ASEA´s state-of-the-art industrial buildings were equipped with new transport systems and other innovations that made work easier.

ASEA transformers, triphase systems, motors, generators, power stations, locomotives etc. were conceived and designed by engineers. These engineers, however, had a much more thorough esthetic education than engineers of today. Many of them had gone to the polytechnic school (in 1946 the Swedish National College of Arts, Crafts and Design), where they had learned to draw, make blueprints, and construct models of high artistic quality. From the 1850s through the first decades of this century, one of the responsibilities of the school was to provide esthetic training for the young people who would later work in industry. These budding engineers were the predecessors of today's industrial designers.

The first generation

It was not by chance that it was at ASEA that the concept of Human Engineering was taken up, by an engineer named John Meilink, or that it was there that the first modern industrial design division, complete with model workshop and the latest equipment, was created in the 1950s. Nor was it by chance that it was another engineer, Rune Zernell at Atlas Copco, who developed an ergonomic approach and ergonomic methodology. Meilink and Zernell were heads of the design divisions at their respective companies.

Of the first generation of industrial designers who regarded themselves as such, many had thus begun as engineers. The incentive came from the United States. Ralph Lysell, who was educated in the U.S., wrote the first article on industrial design published in the Swedish press, in the magazine *Form*, in 1943. A few years later he started the first industrial design consultancy in Stockholm. Many of his employees were engineers, in complete agreement with his philosophy that "a designer should be an engineer first and foremost… and an engineer who knows his subject." In his article in *Form*, he observed that 35 percent of all the new inventions introduced in the United States had actually originated with Swedish engineers. Since there were no industrial designers in Sweden who could transform the inventions into actual products, "these inventions slipped through Swedish hands."

A profession

By the middle of the 1940s, industrial design was becoming an established profession. Sixten Sason worked for Saab, Husqvarna and Electrolux, and Hugo Lindström for the plastics producer Skånska Ättiksfabriken, now Perstorp; he later became the head of the design division at Electrolux. Rune Monö began his career with Sixten Sason at Saab, and subsequently worked for such companies as SAS (where he headed the entire development program); and Per Heribertson's designs included the street lamps that were so admired at the Milan Triennale in 1957. All these men were initially trained as engineers. Stig Lindberg, Sigvard Bernadotte and Astrid Sampe began as artists. A few, including Sigurd Persson, had been silversmiths. They all shared a lively interest in technological development and the potential of the new materials. The results were to be useful to the common man. The concept of More Beautiful Everyday Things was firmly anchored in the Swedish philosophy of industrial design.

The consumer movement in Sweden in the 1940s and 1950s further focused interest on the needs and ideas of the consumer. The industrial designers at Gustavsberg and Electrolux talked with housewives and domestic science teachers and let them test prototypes before production was begun. The Swedish Consumers' Institute developed a solid understanding of physical requirements and ergonomics (although the word itself was not integrated into the Swedish language until the 1960s).

A holistic approach

The holistic approach that so many are talking about today was actually being used back then. The observations of physical therapists and the opinions of doctors, sociological methods such as interviews and questionnaires, time and motion studies, hygiene, function, resource management, needs, usability – all these went into the development of a methodology for product development, from the design of the new Swedish standard kitchen (including the utensils in the kitchen drawer) to the drilling machines at Atlas Copco.

When Sigurd Persson designed Servus, which became Sweden's most popular tableware and was in continuous production for the next 40 years, he literally ate his way to the design – hammered, ate, changed, ate, until he was entirely satisfied. The American concept of "styling" is alien to Swedish design philosophy. It is function, usability, the way it works in actual everyday situations, that is important.

Teaching and learning

In the 1940s and 1950s the open camera was sometimes used to study how people used items or did chores, such as making beds. This was a way to discover the shortcomings in the products. It is in principle the same methodology that Ergonomi Design Gruppen used in its studies of people with reduced mobility in their hands and in the development of new tools for Sandvik Bahco. Video cameras are now used instead of the photographic cameras of that era.

This focus on human needs is also anchored in the education of the 1950s. It was the engineers at the large industries who, in 1957, took the initiative for the first industrial design course at the Swedish National College of Arts, Crafts and Design. The courses, organized by the Swedish Association for Metal Transforming, Mechanical and Electromechanical Engineering Industries and the Society of Swedish Industrial Designers, provided the students with some insight into how engineers and designers in industry thought and what they had to know.

People´s needs

The organizer of the course was John Meilink, an engineer at ASEA. He imprinted the concept of Human Engineering into his students, and in his teaching Louis Sullivan's famous "form follows function" acquired a somewhat different meaning: "Designers should start with people's needs and physical

NEXT PAGE: BICYCLES HAVE BEEN MADE BY ALBERT SAMUELSSON & CO IN SKEPPSHULT FOR OVER 70 YEARS. THE CHARACTERISTIC ROUNDED FORMS OF THE SKEPPSHULT BIKES ECHO THE LINES, COLORS AND DESIGN DETAILS OF THE 1920S. THE BICYCLES ROLL FROM WORKER TO WORKER AND ARE ASSEMBLED BY HAND.

abilities." This was something that the engineers usually didn't think much about, being more concerned with solving construction problems and adapting products to production processes. At Meilink's design division prototypes were developed by specialists in several areas: drafting, model construction etc. This division became the model for some of the design consultancies that were founded in the 1960s, notably Designgruppen and Ergonomidesign, which merged in 1979 to form Ergonomi Design Gruppen. The organization was equipped with a carpenter's workshop, assembly room, machine shop, spray chamber, drafting room, library, photograph studio etc. It was thus possible to produce prototypes that the potential users could test, and then to make precise models for industry. It was also possible to construct full-scale models of workplaces, which was done for Solna Offset – a client since the mid-60s. The assignment was to make the machines in the printing plant safer and easier to operate. Allowing the printers to test full-scale models made it possible to adjust attachments and optimize the placement and design of controls and instrument panels.

The model shop

At most Swedish industrial design offices, the model shop is the heart of operations. It is here the prototypes are developed, and photos and films can then be used to show how the finished product will work and look.

The problems of industrial workplaces began to interest industrial designers, especially the students at the Swedish National College of Arts, Crafts and Design, in the late 60s. Heavy lifting, hazardous, awkward working positions, monotonous, repetitive movements, dangerous machines – all this was considered a question of poor design, a lack of Human Engineering.

In recent years both design students and working industrial designers have begun to address the problems of workers in hospitals and health care, where heavy lifts and poorly designed equipment are everyday phenomena. Complicated machines can be a source of uncertainty, and an ambiguously designed control panel can become a question of life or death. In the increasingly high-tech world of medical care, with ultrasound, lasers and computer tomography, both Human Engineering and aggressive intervention are needed to protect the patient's quality of life.

Technology/innovation, design and economics – each of these three pillars is by tradition an education unto itself, in an engineering school, a design institute or a business college. However, a collaboration between the Royal Institute of Technology and the Swedish National College of Arts, Crafts and Design was begun in the late 1960s. Some of these future engineers and industrial designers arrived at a completely new design for a garbage truck and an idea for simplifying garbage collection and disposal in cities.

Learning from each other

In 1980 the university in Luleå advertised a professorship in industrial ergonomics. The appointed professor was an industrial designer, which can be seen as an indication that the importance of the industrial designer's contribution to the product development process was recognized.

In recent years the Royal Institute of Technology, the Swedish University College of Arts, Crafts and Design and the Stockholm School of Economics have drawn closer together, and have tried to learn from each other's methodologies, language and ways of thinking.

In the 1980s it was common in Sweden, as elsewhere, to speak of the importance of design in marketing and in establishing a company's image. But the hero worship surrounding designers in some other countries has so far not been seen in Sweden. The concept of economy, in the form of optimum use of resources and energy, is part of traditional Swedish culture.

The job of the designer is to achieve a more effective, leaner production. A more moral attitude seems to have returned to Sweden in the 1990s. A designer who considers only the surface, the color and shape, is simply not professional. It is no longer possible to neglect ecological aspects and use environmentally hazardous materials, or to ignore obvious practical requirements of the manufacturers or the users. The design ethic and the concept of Human Engineering that developed during the 1950s are having a renaissance. A few years ago Oscar Tusquets, a Spanish architect and industrial designer, observed ironically that "Swedish industrial designers are the world's Boy Scouts." When they heard this, Swedish designers responded "What's the matter with Boy Scouts? Boy Scouts defend democracy and promote understanding between people. They learn to manage comfortably in the wilderness with a minimum of resources."

Wasn't this the way the first design was once created? A stone was carefully chipped, and became an axe, which made life better and more secure: Human Engineering.

NEXT PAGE:
THE TURBO GTG 40. ATLAS COPCO'S NEW GRINDER, IS THE FIRST TO BE POWERED WITH A TURBINE ENGINE. VIBRATION IS MINIMIZED WITH THE AUTO BALANCER. DESIGN BY ROLF JACOBSSON.

33

A COMMERCIAL HUMANISM

BY
ULF MANNERVIK

In the new society that is emerging, greater demands are made on industrial design. In particular, society's resources must be used in a responsible way. For our increasingly complex environment to become as uncomplicated as possible, we must develop a holistic approach that focuses on the user. This is a necessity if we are to have control over our lives in the future. And this is an exciting challenge for Swedish user-friendly design.

The industrial society is currently facing sweeping changes. The primary reason for these changes is very rapid development in applications of electronics.

To a greater extent than ever before, enormous and growing complexity demands a holistic view of society and our own role in it, as well as the role of our possessions. It is not enough to understand the most efficient way to respond in the new society; we must also know how to do the least possible ecological damage.

It becomes more difficult to perceive the whole as the pace of developments accelerates, with lead times shrinking and compatible competence becoming increasingly mobile. These changes demand a better understanding of core competence and the building of efficient networks in order to share in, and deal with, the competencies of suppliers, competitors and customers.

The competitive strength of a company depends on its ability to create added value for its customers and itself by specialization and collaboration with other actors in its field of operation.

Swedish industrial designers have such a specialization in their focus on user-friendliness, since companies today are increasingly customer-oriented.

Environmental awareness and a holistic view in the development of products are to some extent characteristic of Swedish design today. Swedish industrial designers have also begun to perceive the value of building strong networks with competitors as well as with other actors in the market.

Design and competition

Design has great significance for companies, since it adds value and thus competitive strength to products. The concept of design here refers to the activities the companies use to visualize or create physical structures in order to offer products and services to customers. Good design in this respect can be said to be short-term and long-term competitive combinations of esthetics, technology and marketing. Design becomes standardized in today´s industrial nations. Different forms of design are appropriate for different parts of the market and different phases of a company´s development. But if knowledge can be developed around a unique, core competence in the company, with its own distinct design characteristics, this core competence can constitute a resource for diffentiation that can be used when such is needed. This applies equally to individual companies and to larger organizational or regional groupings.

Global differentiation

Increasing numbers of modern, progressive, industrial nations have realized that design can be brought a further step forward by safeguarding, fostering and refining specific national characteristics. A unique design culture creates a valuable opportunity for differentiation, since cultural factors change slowly and are difficult for outsiders to imitate. It is therefore of particular interest to develop cultural factors as core competencies. The relatively durable nature of these factors, however, does not eliminate the need to develop the ability to readily adapt them to the rapid changes of our epoch.

The importance of regional or cultural peculiarities may also increase with the new era's global flow of capital, people, ideas and technology. As changes become more far-reaching, not only the ability to adapt but also each culture's or region's more durable and unique core qualities will become important. Information technology and other infrastructure that facilitates this flow will probably accelerate this tendency.

Swedish differentiation

The core competence in Swedish design today is user-friendliness. The value of this competence increases as it becomes increasingly important to be able to create and offer complex products to customers, but which are not, because of their complexity, more complicated to use.

In Sweden, industrial designers have been concentrating on how to adapt products to the user's specific context for decades. After much specifically targeted development work,

Swedish design has built up a substantial competence in this area. User-friendliness is based on an old Swedish cultural tradition of consideration and respect for the individual in society. In terms of esthetics, we have a heritage that we have now recognized the importance of developing.

It is important, however, to emphasize that specifically Swedish design is neither an isolated phenomenon nor a universal solution for all products and all markets. Its qualities are also found in other design cultures, though perhaps not in the same combinations. The Swedish design tradition has developed and is still developing in national as well as international contexts. Uniquely Swedish design is also a means of differentiation. Its qualities are aimed at, and mostly suited to that part of the market that values user-friendliness, safety, timelessness and a pared-down elegance, but this obviously makes it less suited to markets that do not put a premium on these qualities.

Tradition and development

To put it simply, two different forms of design in two different markets have contributed to Swedish competitive strength during the past century.

The first is found in Swedish Grace from the 1920s, with artistically refined handicrafts

of high quality or with small-scale series production for a small group of reasonably wealthy buyers. This has reverberations in the Swedish post-modern design of the 1980s, with such items as furniture made in small, numbered editions. This is an example of elitist design of primarily esthetic value. The product as an expression in itself is central, rather than its function and the adaptation of its form to how the product will be used. The other type of design is reflected in the concept "More Beautiful Everyday Things." Functionalism and modernism during the 1920s, 1930s and 1940s, and the focus in recent years on ergonomics, safety and minorities in society, have in common that the utilization of the products is the focus. Thus, more than a well-to-do elite can participate in raising both the aesthetic and usage-related value of the product which Swedish design has the potential to provide. This means a better use of resources than if the product has primarily esthetic qualities. But this does not mean that its esthetic values are negligible or not worth striving for.

The two types of design have, of course, different areas of application, and are not mutually exclusive, but the latter can probably contribute most to the competitive strength of Swedish industry.

The demand for Swedish design that has now been awakened is largely due to the knowledge about user-friendliness that Swedish industrial designers have developed in recent times. It is not a mute nostalgia based on our former esthetic glory, but instead has developed from an earlier context.

In the early 1980s, Sweden made a name for itself with its products for people with disabilities and other vulnerable groups, such as the elderly. The Swedish understanding of how to adapt products to older people is of special interest since these markets are now growing rapidly and require their own solutions in the form of products and services.

The unique character of Swedish design lies in its consideration for the individual and in its purity and honesty of expression. It is relaxingly straightforward functional design, free from extravagant gestures, with a pared-down design language that seeks to emphasize what is necessary with elegance.

The latter is rapidly becoming more important as society becomes increasingly complex. The considerable contributions that high technology have made to development are based on its ability to create complex systems, but in order to master these, the user must be able to understand them. For the user's sake, we have to create uncomplicated complexity. This is an important area of development in which Swedish design's focus on the user and his conditions becomes an interesting possibility.

Commercial humanism

Design has periodically been regarded as a commercial tool for seducing and duping the consumer. This is how it was during the late 1960s and early 1970s. Similar attitudes and trends are seen in today's anti-design movement. However, this movement risks becoming just as cynically polarized as the current overwhelming and largely cosmetic ecological trend.

Just as individual companies are now faced with the choice of either cultivating their highest quality skills and integrating these into a larger external context, or letting them wither away, we have to work for a design that wisely takes advantage of the resources a company has at its disposal. These resources are its total capital, including financial capital, production capital, human capital (knowledge), market capital (collaboration, players that develop the company), and ecological capital. We have to have a nuanced view of the necessary interplay between these different types of capital. Otherwise we are doomed to a destructive oscillating between utopian extremes.

Design has to be put into a context where its intentions are furthered by being articulated, rather than by being hidden. Only in such a commercial system can a "human" design become established. The Swedish design of today is a promising step in this direction, as long as the honesty of the design does not evolve into meddlesomeness and its pared-downness does not translate into the maiming of the end in itself.

For parts of a market, there is a commercial potential in the qualities of Swedish design, and this guarantees that the Swedish development of The Human Dimension of design can continue to develop in collaboration with national and international players.

NEXT PAGE:
WHEN EINAR HAREIDE AND AINA NILSSON DESIGNED THE SAAB 900 CONVERTIBLE, THEIR GUIDELINES WERE "NOTHING EXTREME, FADDISH, HARD OR AGGRESSIVE."

THE USER'S VIEWPOINT AS TOOL

BY
OLLE BOBJER
ROLAND KADEFORS
ÅSA KILBOM
LENA SPERLING

hand tools have for a long time been a serious problem in manufacturing industries, particularly for workers who are women. Researchers, users, industrial designers and manufacturers are cooperating to find a solution. Through their dialog, the perspectives have widened and new problems have been debated. Ten prototypes of better hand tools will be ready at the end of 1994. This co-operation is to continue with a review of hand-held machines.

A long with hearing and eyesight, the hand is man's most important contact with the outside world. Loss of hand function is considered to severely impair our ability to perform the normal activities of daily life.

The most important aspects of the hand´s function are its sensitivity, its ability to exert force and its mobility. Almost no other part of the human body is so richly supplied with sensory nerve endings as the hand. Nerve endings, especially in the palm and the fingertips, permit us to identify the subtle differences in surface textures, and the pressure and friction from materials and tools. Think about the hand's ability to read Braille. This finely developed sensitivity is a prerequisite for precision and speed in the exertion of force.

In some manual tasks, the hand is used for repeated forceful gripping, pushing and pulling up to 80 percent of the time. However, sustained activity of this kind can easily cause injury to the hand, no matter how strong it is, resulting in pain and inflammation in the joints and tendons, nerve impairment with reduced sensitivity for precision work, and reduced endurance. In other words, both suffering and loss of productivity are the result.

In the majority of manual tasks, the hand works with a tool, and the design of this tool significantly influences the demands made on the hand. With optimally designed tools, these demands can be reduced and the ability to perform precision work can be improved.

Hand function and the risks for stress injuries have been studied at the Swedish National Institute of Occupational Health in a series of experimental and epidemiological studies. The physiological demands and the nature of musculoskeletal disorders from working with hand tools and vibrating machines have been measured as a basis for redesigning the tools.

The user as critic

In the Stone Age, people used their creative abilities to make simple tools, using simple methods, for their own hands and their own work. New needs and greater demands resulted in new ways of using, designing and making hand tools. The user now ordered tools from a craftsman, who made them and was familiar with the demands that the user, and the contexts of its use, placed on each of his creations. The user was no longer the maker, but was still the orderer. Industrialization increased the need for functional tools. There were new possibilities of mass-producing tools.

The distance between the user and the maker increased, and a gap arose between knowledge and its practical application.

The most welcome tools have their roots in practical needs. It is the user who is the expert on the context in which the tool is used, and who accepts or rejects the new product.

It is important to develop a close relationship with the users. It is only in such a context that it is possible to access the unarticulated knowledge that the professional more or less unconsciously bears and applies in his work.

Ergonomic research has generated quite an amount of knowledge that is yet to be put to any practical use. In Sweden, research into the ergonomics of the hand has provided a solid foundation for the continued development of good hand tools.

Ask a professional

Using a hand tool comes naturally to a professional. His mind is usually on solving problems, meeting specifications and achieving good results. He usually does not pay much attention to how the tool is being used.

However, this kind of information is necessary if a tool is to be designed so that it is as good as it can be. Tools are also used in unconventional and possibly even non-permitted ways. It is also important to know about this kind of usage when new tools are being designed, since unconventional usage indicates a need for a design different than the original tool, for a slightly different purpose.

There are plenty of hand tools on the market. One way to push development forward is to ask professionals to appraise the tools that are presently considered the best, and also let them criticize bad tools.

An experimental model

Most workers have a difficult time answering the question of how they would like to improve a tool.

It is therefore more efficient to produce a number of different and in some cases radically different tools, that can be the starting point for discussion; or function as idea stimulators in in-depth interviews with professionals.

These interviews provide the basis for making a limited number of tools which the professional worker can use and assess, not only from the point of view of ergonomics, but also technical capability. How workers use the tools is registered using objective methods, e.g. wrist position, angle of the hand and elbow, how long and how often they are used, and how much force is needed. The operator can also rank each tool's characteristics and performance subjectively, using estimation scales for different variables, and estimating the physical effort required. A large number of characteristics are registered for each worker that tries out the prototypes, e.g., hand measurements, maximum grip strength, age, height, weight, professional experience. This information is used to be able to compare the results with measurements for the intended users. At the same time, information is

generated on whether several different sizes are needed (small, medium and large), or gearing or servo assistance, so that the tool can be used without risk of injury.

A functional model

With ergonomic requirements as the basis, detailed discussions are held with engineers at manufacturing companies on the possibilities of achieving desired functions while retaining the quality and durability of the tool. Companies that have respect for the ergonomic approach are often prepared to develop materials and manufacturing techniques to meet these requirements. A thorough ergonomic analysis results in strongly weighted arguments in discussions with design engineers and production engineers.

The series of functional models is then made with surface treatment and coloring the same as for production-ready samples. Professionals are permitted to use these models for a period of time in their normal work and appraise them so that the industrial designer can make final judgements concerning the tool´s ergonomic function and technical characteristics, and provide the marketing department with ideas about future sales.

The user in focus

Sweden's largest engineering industries joined Swedish forces in 1992 and received support from the Swedish Working Life Fund to replace the ten "worst" hand tools with new products. A strong contributing factor was that research results could be directly given a practical application. Users, researchers, manufacturers and distributors would be part of the project from the beginning to the end, and the user was to be its focus. The project began with the various parties involved coming to an agreement on the criteria defining a problem tool.

A large inventory of problem tools at the various engineering companies was made, with the users of these tools providing the major input. Several hundred questionnaires were returned to the project. They described the tools, the situations in which they are used, and who the users are, as well as the types of problem associated with them. A list of the 20 "worst" and most common problem tools was made up and became the focus for the remainder of the project.

At least one company using each problem tool was visited and usage of the tool was filmed. Users were interviewed about the tool´s characteristics. Its quality was also assessed, in order to bring out comments and requirements, and ideas for improvements.

Users' requirements could thus be specified and became their orders for new tools.

For the highest priority tool, namely the workshop hammer, there were special requirements:
- The design of the handle/shaft
- Balance

- The surface treatment of the handle/shaft
- The striking surfaces.

Researchers supplemented the user´s requirements with scientifically based ergonomic requirements for hammers, and current standards. This requirements specification was then used as the basis for the development of prototypes.

The design group tested the alternative hammers with the help of users. The test models were used to systematically develop a final prototype with the help of the users. This prototype was thus the concrete realization of what the users wanted. The prototype's ergonomic characteristics were then evaluated in a special hand tool laboratory. Measurement methods were developed to verify the set ergonomic requirements.

A 0-series of products will then be tested for a longer period by professional users. A tool can only be considered good after it has become accepted by professional users in their work.

To reduce the obstacles that exist along the road from manufacturer to user, all interested parties must understand the importance of selling and buying good hand tools. With the help of Tool Facts, a system for testing and information, good hand tools can be produced and bad products can be gradually forced off the market.

NEXT PAGE:
Xᵀᴴ TRIENNALE, MILANO 1954, THE SWEDISH EXHIBITION.

SWEDEN RETURNS TO ITALY

BY
ANTY PANSERA

Sweden has returned to the Palazzo dell'Arte in the true sense of the word, or more correctly, it has returned to the Triennale. Its history with this exhibition may be described as long, unbroken and at times particularly significant. Its relationship with the Milanese exhibition body existed long before the transfer from the Villa Reale in Monza to the Palazzo dell'Arte in Milan.

Official participations span from 1923 to 1992 (with unofficial ones in 1927, 1930 and 1940), illustrating just how important Sweden considers this appointment. This exhibition can be compared to the qualifying round for promotion and diffusion of the applied arts and artistic craftwork, to be followed by industrial production to include products and articles in a wider distribution network.

However, in some events of the more recent past, adhesion to themes proposed by the Triennale also presented the opportunity for a contribution based on analysis and reflection on the project the exhibition was hosting.

Swedish Modern design

Without a doubt, "Swedish style" has been placed on almost mythical levels in Italy: it has been promoted in Italy since the 1950s by the leading Italian press – *Domus* can be considered representative – which described Sweden as the "mother of the entire Scandinavian movement for the applied arts."

There has been a lively curiosity about Northern countries – Scandinavia in particular – since before the last World War. Ignazio Gardella recalls a trip he made with Giuseppe Pagano in 1939. They wanted to do some research on design and production methods in these Northern countries and see first-hand what lessons could be learnt: during this trip they met with two of the leading architects of that time, Alvar Aalto and Gunnar Asplund. Their curiosity had been stimulated by the appearance of high quality products for everyday use, which everyone could afford, thanks to modern technology and mass production. The articles were easily identifiable by their form and by the use of natural materials in their manufacture. Furniture, utensils, decorative accessories: a collection which, according to Vittorio Gregotti, was described by the young architects and designers of the 1950s as "homely, quiet, understated, anti-demonstrative, definitely Social Democratic," and presented a possible "alternative to repetition of specific historical identity, using the tradition of modernity in the wides possible context."

Apart from cultural renewal, furnishing a home "Swedish style" was seen almost as a political statement, in line with the connection between Swedish modernism and moralism emphasized by numerous historians of the country: this choice, strangely enough, was not exclusive to the intellectuals, but widened to embrace everyone who wished to "update" his own personal taste and way of life.

Respect for nature

Articles and materials in harmony with a respect for nature and man helped coin the phrase "modernism with a human aspect." Even today, it is the subject of this event with its self-explanatory title.

The theme is strongly linked to the local traditions which represented Sweden's contribution to the First Biennale, held in Monza in 1923; on this occasion, the curators noted that "the formula of the so-called modern styles never had much luck in Sweden. Because of the climate, the population has to live indoors for most of the year and as a result the passion for the home has become almost a religion."

Along with the articles exhibited, there were reconstructions of interiors: a scullery kitchen by Carl Malmsten – a traditionalist who in the 1940s began producing furniture for the mass markets, alongside an exclusive line of hand-made artisanal pieces – and a dining room by Carl Horvik, both illustrating a balanced sense of modernity.

The articles designed by Simon Gate and Edward Hald, presented in 1927 were acclaimed as "perfect examples of good taste, right equilibrium and perfect manufacture," as was the "small, high-class, tasteful selection presented in 1930 alongside crystal and pewter" later proposed by Florent Robert in 1936 and again in 1940 as a perfect example of the evolution in taste.

Rebuilding

The "Triennale della Ricostruzione" (The Triennale exhibition on rebuilding) of 1947 co-ordinated by Piero Bottoni, had a single theme: the home, "the most realistic theme, the most heartfelt and the most dramatic, a subject of anxiety, desire and hope for millions of Europeans." Under the supervision of an organizing committee headed by Elof Eriksson and art director Bengt Gate, Sweden presented its own field of furniture manufacture. The problems of building and rebuilding were analogous: massive immigration into the cities; the desire to "try to improve the standards of homes both in the town and in the country" was obvious.

In the entry for the IXth Triennale, organized by Erik Wettergren, Gotthard Johansson and Bengt Gate, there was a return to "decorative and industrial art": glass, ceramics and textiles were featured alongside metal objects and furniture, all characterized by the use of natural materials, by lightness of structure and by form.

At the Xth Triennale (1954) on the themes of "prefabrication, unification and industrial design," the Swedish section, supervised by Eva Benedicks and the architects Sven Engström and Gunnar Myrstrand, responded with the reconstruction of a "Swedish corner on Italian soil." *Domus* acknowledged its success by acclaiming Sweden as "a huge laboratory of applied art which really

NEXT PAGE:
TOP: VIIITH TRIENNALE, MILANO 1947, THE SWEDISH KITCHEN BY HSB.
BOTTOM: XITH TRIENNALE, MILANO 1957, THE SWEDISH LIVING ROOM.

functions; it seemed like the entire country was working in the field...." Public interest was equal to that of the previous year, when La Rinascente – the huge Milanese department store dedicated to "quality" – presented an area exclusively for Swedish designer goods for everyday use.

However, the Swedish contribution to that year's Triennale was dedicated to single pieces of furniture and to the exhibition of industrial design (which was supervised by Achille and Pergiacomo Castiglioni, Roberto Menghi, Augusto Morello, Marcello Nizzoli, Michele Provinciali and Alberto Rosselli) and the historical retrospective which told the story of "30 years of the Triennale." Works by Simon Gate, Edward Hald, Vicke Lindstrand and Edwin Öhrström were presented.

The XIth Triennale, in 1957, again showed the discerning choice of Eva Benedicks (the section was organized by Åke H. Huldt): glass and steel as finished products were deliberately selected to be associated with "Swedish design." The items emphasized perfection of form, but each illustrated the combination of "the fantasy of its creator, craftwork and industrial precision."

Examples of Scandinavian design also appeared at the "International Exhibition of Modern Architecture," where works of various architects, from Gunnar Asplund to Sven Ivar Lind, were presented. These bore witness to the subtle changes in the conception of the urban environment, illustrated by building projects in Gothenburg in 1940, Lidingö in 1945-46 and Uppsala in 1952, by Stig Axel Ancker, Bengt Gate and Sten Lindegren. Then in the "International Exhibition of the Home," as an example of a typical abode, Gustaf Rosenberg presented a living room for a house built in the outskirts of Stockholm: the items he used were all readily available on the market.

Swedish glass and steel re-appeared at the international exhibition in 1960 dedicated to these two materials. The themes of the XIIth Triennale were "home and school" and Sweden's contribution was supervised by Eva Benedicks and Hans Asplund. Some school buildings were designed for the event, and for the home easily accessible articles were presented, with particular attention to textiles and ceramics.

Experimentalism

Sweden was absent from the XIIIth Triennale held in 1964 on leisure time, but returned in 1968 (XIVth Triennale dedicated to "mass production") with an attempt to illustrate and analyze the current transformations in society and the contemporary environment, and gave some predictions on the future. The Swedish division (supervised by Bo Wingren, Sture Balgard and Jöran Lindvall), was dedicated to the enormous expansion of possibilities offered by Western society: the impossibility of comprehending and dominating the innumerable and complex phenomena of production and the difficulty of achieving a synthesis can only lead to "perennial experimentalism" and in the city to "perennial transformation."

A hall was fitted with a number of screens for the non-stop projection of about 3000 images, with electronic background music composed specially by Ralph Lundsten and Leo Nilson. The phenomenon of serial production was given particular attention, not only its technical aspects but also its economic, commercial, social, psychological and environmental ones. This subject was the basis of an operation which was perfected in 1973 for the XVth Triennale, "high-lighting the existing relationship and the desirable one between children or teenagers and the environment, and documenting new situations predicted to arise when it is their turn to influence it." Sweden, Denmark, Finland and Norway joined forces in this project (supervised by Lennart Lindkvist). Balls of different sizes and a group of 19 children (by the Finnish sculptress Rauni Liukka) were placed in a large rectangular area with lowered ceilings and black walls. The children were depicted engrossed in play or other activities. Panels along the walls provided a photographic commentary on the "current situations of childhood." The contribution, described as "fundamentally ideological," compared the existing situations with the desirable ones. This theme provided the basis for the "Swedish fairy tale" – a provocative reconstruction of a traditional home, supervised by Thomas Hellquist and Bianca Heymowska for the XVIIIth Trien-nale, in 1992. The entry was well in tune with the exhibition's main theme "Life among objects and nature: design and the challenge of the environment." The selected "specimens" originated from different eras and "classes," from the world of pure architecture, art and design.

From culture to nature

From culture to nature once again: the mediator is Man, the prime user of the habitat, getting both materials and inspiration from nature. With these he constructed a culture which was artificial at first, but which today is one of reality and basic values, aptly summarized in the title of this exhibition: The Human Dimension.

Another revision/proposal – an invitation to analysis and thought – which may give rise to a suitable procedural and design pathway: this route will extend from home design (which has been a focus of attention in the past) to encompass our entire habitat.

PAGE 57: THE WORK CLOTHES AVAILABLE IN 1925 WORE OUT QUICKLY AND OFTEN INCREASED THE RISK OF ACCIDENT, SO JOHN MAGNUSSON (1892–1992) BEGAN TO MAKE CLOTHES, CONCENTRATING ON QUALITY, COMFORT AND GOOD FIT. THE CLOTH IS STILL WOVEN IN FRISTAD'S OWN FACTORIES.

PAGE 58: TREATMENT WITH THE GROWTH HORMONE GENOTROPIN ENTAILS DAILY INJECTIONS OVER MANY YEARS. WITH THE GENOTROPIN KABI PEN, TAKING INJECTIONS IS SIMPLE AND CONVENIENT.

PAGE 59: NINE OF TEN PATIENTS WHO GET A NEW HIP JOINT REGAIN THEIR MOBILITY COMPLETELY. THE OPERATION TAKES A COUPLE OF HOURS. THE ARTIFICIAL HIP JOINTS ARE MADE BY MITAB WITH STEEL FROM SANDVIK.

PAGE 60: ENVIRONMENT-FRIENDLY PRODUCTION IS THE WATCHWORD FOR BÖLEBYNS GARVERI AB, WHERE SKINS ARE TANNED WITH BARK INSTEAD OF CHROME SALTS. THE LEATHER IS USED FOR SHOES, BACKPACKS, BRIEFCASES AND HUNTING ACCESSORIES.

PAGE 61: GRÄNSFORS AXES ARE MASTERPIECES OF CRAFTSMANSHIP. WHEN THE SMITH IS SATISFIED WITH HIS WORK, HE STAMPS HIS INITIALS INTO THE AXEHEAD. GRÄNSFORS AXES WON A PRIZE FOR ECOLOGICAL DESIGN IN A COMPETITION HELD IN 1990 BY THE SWEDISH SOCIETY OF CRAFTS AND DESIGN AND THE SWEDISH SOCIETY FOR THE CONSERVATION OF NATURE.

PAGE 62: THIS PEN IS DESIGNED FOR ARTHRITICS AND OTHER PEOPLE WHO HAVE TROUBLE BENDING THEIR FINGERS. IT FITS COMFORTABLY AGAINST THE BASE OF THE THUMB, AND CAN BE FILLED WITH LEAD SHOT TO MAKE IT HEAVIER. THE PEN, DEVELOPED BY DESIGN KONSULTERNA, IS MARKETED BY RFSU REHAB.

PAGE 63: SAS ORDERED A BETTER COFFEEPOT. LOCATING THE HANDLE CLOSER TO THE CENTER OF GRAVITY MADE IT POSSIBLE FOR CABIN PERSONNEL TO POUR WITHOUT BENDING THEIR WRISTS. ERGONOMI DESIGN GRUPPEN CAME UP WITH THE IDEA.

PAGE 64: AN ERGONOMICALLY DESIGNED TOOL AND A GOOD GRIP CAN REDUCE THE RISK OF OCCUPATIONAL INJURY. THESE ELECTRICAN'S PLIERS ARE ALSO USED WITH ELECTRONICS, AND ARE MADE BY PRESSMASTER TOOL. DESIGNED BY MIKAEL NILSSON AND ERGONOMI DESIGN GRUPPEN.

PAGE 65: ATLAS COPCO'S LONG TRADITION OF ERGONOMIC DESIGN IS HERE EXEMPLIFIED BY THE DEVELOPMENT OF HAND-HELD TOOLS FROM 1915 TO 1984.

PAGE 66: OUTDOOR CLOTHING AND EQUIPMENT ARE TESTED IN BITING COLD. KLÄTTERMUSEN SPORTSWEAR IS DESIGNED BY LALLA ERSARE, WHO KNOWS FROM LONG EXPERIENCE HOW RAPIDLY THE WEATHER CAN CHANGE IN SWEDEN'S NORTHERN WILDERNESS.

PAGE 67: PLAYGROUND EQUIPMENT SHOULD BE FUN TO PLAY ON, BUT IT SHOULD ALSO BE SAFE. THE OLD-STYLE CLIMBING NETS HAD SMALL HOLES, AND A CHILD COULD GET STUCK. THE NEW NETS HAVE LARGER HOLES AND ELIMINATE THIS RISK.

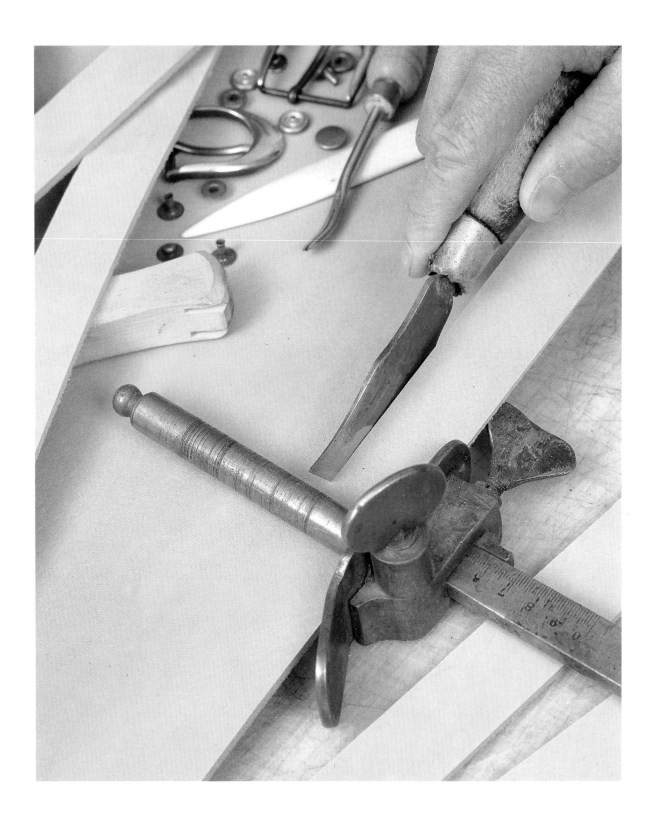

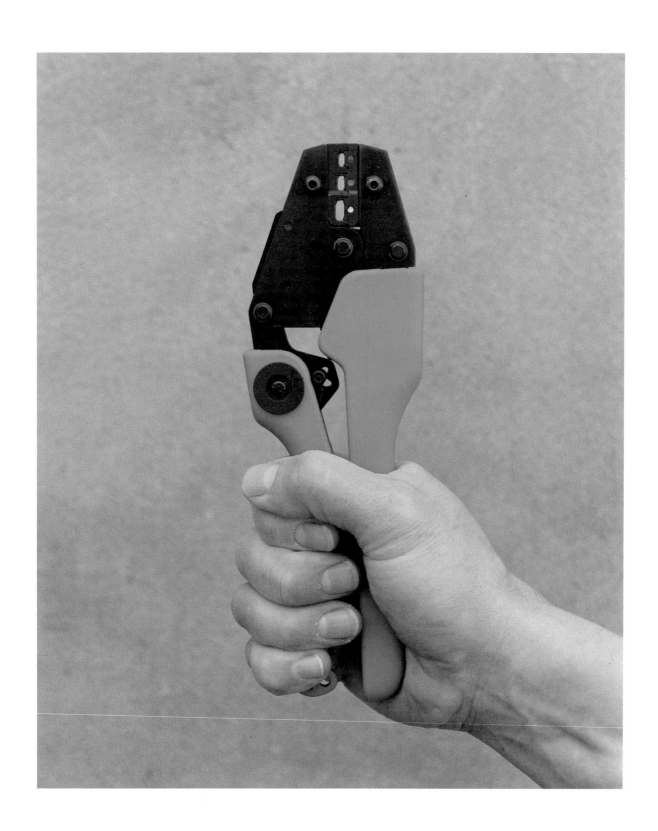

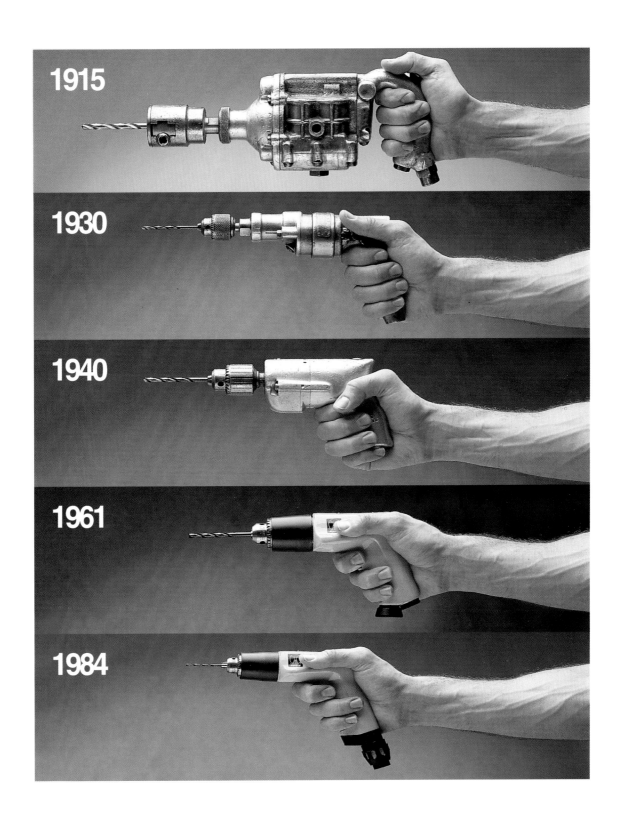

care and caring

BY
MARIA BENKTZON

PHOTO: NICE ENOUGH FOR A FORMAL
DINNER. RFSU REHAB, WORKING
WITH ERGONOMI DESIGN GRUPPEN,
HAS DEVELOPED UTENSILS, PLATES
AND GLASSES FOR PEOPLE WHO HAVE
TROUBLE GRASPING AND LIFTING
ORDINARY TABLEWARE.

CARE AND CARING

BY MARIA BENKTZON

We started with esthetics, not function, when we began to design aids for people with disabilities. Nobody knew much about function. The tools designed for the disabled were often clumsy and ugly. The Swedish concept therefore became to design simple, beautiful everyday utensils that nobody would be ashamed of and want to hide in a drawer.

Being able to cut and eat food. Being able to take care of personal hygiene – brushing teeth, bathing, going to the toilet. These things are very important to a person's wellbeing – spiritual and mental as well as physical.

The international standing of Swedish design in this area is not due to the fact *that* designers have worked with aids, but to *how* they worked. Sweden was one of the first to unite esthetics with function, making esthetics an important part of the design of many utensils and aids.

The overall goal is that people with disabilities should be integrated into society, and live their lives as independently as possible. It is possible to modify buildings so that they are accessible to more people, and to design products so that more people can use them. Target groups can be expanded to include people whose abilities have been reduced by age, injury or disease. There are several different terms for this concept, including "design for a broader average," "universal design," "design for people at all stages of their lives" and "trans-generational design." "Design for a broader average" best describes the Swedish approach.

This requires fairly comprehensive design research – studies of grip and motion patterns, for example. It may be a matter of finding a form that suits more people than the one currently being used. The design process must start from the physical abilities of the user, and these are non-negotiable. This is not to say that one form can suit everyone, however; more may be required, or even several different ones. The important thing is to see the opportunities in the limitations, and this applies to the forms also – and not only for the eye, but for the other senses as well. Ergonomics is more than physical comfort, and esthetics is more than visual beauty.

Aids to independence

The principle is to develop products that make the most of the user's resources. The utensils should compensate for the user's reduced abilities, make an activity easier, maybe even make an impossible activity possible. Another purpose may be to prevent injuries, perhaps by eliminating movements that would place stress on inflamed joints. What strengths and abilities do we attribute to the potential user when we start to design a new workplace, tool or utensil?

Workers at Ergonomi Design Gruppen have developed a range of knives with angled handles. Many people with arthritis find it difficult to cut with an ordinary knife. Stiff joints, poor grip and reduced muscular strength can make the necessary motions painful or even impossible. If the wrist is instead slightly bent and the fingers can close into a fist around the handle, the maximum strength of the hand can be used and even a person with weak hands can cut. These saw knives can be used by everyone, but for precision work an ordinary straight knife is better.

Knives, forks and spoons with thick handles are another example. Many people consider them clumsy-looking, but the dimensions and the weight are necessary to the function. This tableware is designed for people who have difficulty closing their hands. It is impossible to hold a thin handle with fingers that will not bend. There should therefore be a range of tableware with handles of different thicknesses, and the thinner ones can be used by others. Making things easier to hold and use also makes it possible for more people to use them.

Changes in design and size are not always as striking as with the angled knives or the thick-handled tableware. If a utensil or work tool is used long or often, even small details in design can have considerable effect on efficiency, comfort and safety.

Workers at Ergonomi Design Gruppen have designed butcher knives, pliers, toothbrushes and other utensils. A layman may find it difficult to see that these work better, but it becomes obvious once they are tried out. The knife handle is designed for the nine grips most commonly used in butchering.

The toothbrush handle, which comes in two different sizes, works well for both nondisabled people and those with reduced strength and flexibility in their hands. The handle can be fixed in several different positions, so that the brush can reach all parts of the mouth and it is not necessary to bend the wrist or lift the elbow and shoulder.

The angled kitchen knives and the thick-handled tableware, with their hard geometric lines, are designs of the 1970s. The forms of the 90s are softer, more organic. The goal has been to make an esthetically appealing synthesis of form and function that is gentle and reserved.

The user as designer

To obtain good results, it is necessary to extract as much as possible from the experience of the users. By having people with different physical abilities, ages and sex try different designs, ergonomics becomes a natural part of development work. Working with those who will use the products also increases understanding for the differences in people's ways of using them.

Ergonomi Design Gruppen was asked, for example, to develop an ergonomically better coffeepot for SAS. Redesigning the handle and moving it closer to the pot's center of gravity made it possible to work with a straight wrist. The grip can be firmer, and the serving safer. Practical tests with cabin personnel showed that the load on the arm and wrist was considerably lessened. Stainless steel inside the spout increases durability and helps to stop drips. The pot was developed to improve working conditions for people with normal hand function, but it has also been found to be practical for people with reduced strength and flexibility in their arms and hands. Knowledge from one area was transferred to another, and the sphere of people who benefit from the solution was expanded.

 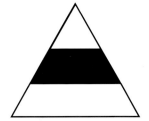 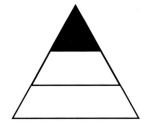

The user pyramid

The user's abilities and limitations are an important starting point in developing a new product. This attitude toward the design process can be illustrated with a user pyramid. The pyramid represents all conceivable users, their abilities to manage daily activities, and the ways these abilities are affected by illness, injury and old age.

At the base of the pyramid are non-handicapped people and older people with slight disabilities, such as a bit of stiffness or some deterioration in strength, sight or hearing. In the middle part of the pyramid are people with more serious disabilities due to illness or age: those who need aids in order to move around, or are visually impaired, for example. This group includes many older people and most of the ten percent of the population that can be classified as disabled. If their surroundings were adapted to their physical abilities, most of them would be able to manage with little or no assistance.

At the top of the pyramid are people with severe disabilities, those who need help with many daily activities: certain wheelchair users, for example, or people with very little strength or mobility in arms or hands. Many of them can not hold things with their hands. This group includes people such as the world-famous British physicist Stephen Hawking, who can make valuable contributions to society despite their disabilities.

It is important to consider and respect these people. Since the demands placed on the products become greater toward the top of the pyramid, the result often is that more people are able to use them. Two illustrative examples are photoelectric cells that automatically open doors and centrally operated door locks on cars, which are necessary for some people but make life easier for others. The angled knife, the toothbrush and the coffeepot are other examples of expanding the sphere of potential users.

NEXT PAGE:
ASSEMBLING AN IKEA CHAIR IS A FAMILY MATTER. THIS ONE, DESIGNED BY TOMAS JELINEK, IS IN IKEA'S CLASSIC STOCKHOLM LINE.

more beautiful everyday things

BY
GUNILLA LUNDAHL

BY GUNILLA LUNDAHL

*t*he term "Vackrare Vardagsvara," More Beautiful Everyday Things, was coined in 1919 by Gregor Paulson, a leading figure in Swedish design for several decades. Behind the ideas he outlined in a brochure of the Society of Swedish Industrial Designers lay years of highly successful collaboration between the Society and Swedish industry, in which placements were arranged for artists in the industrial production process. In this context design was a matter of holistic solutions, not a question of style alone.

"*Vackrare Vardagsvara*" was a concept that came to color and permeate the Swedish attitude and approach to design, and to give it its unique character.

The everyday, and the work that gave it meaning, was the focus of Paulson's ideas. Beauty could also be found in the everyday, as an essential quality. Beauty should not be like a party frock, put on for special occasions only. When *Vackrare Vardagsvara* was written, Sweden was still a poor country that, in its better moments, managed to elevate poverty to a teacher and frugality to a virtue. Being able to economize was a necessary skill in those days, without this necessarily excluding a streak of poetry, delicately symbolized by the simple, wild briar rose. This simplicity was supported by a sense of proportion and a feeling for good design and the right material. It was a necessity to use resources well.

Industrialized Sweden at that time was still close to the old agricultural society with its artisanal traditions and its sense of how things should feel in the hand – how they should appeal to all the senses. This heritage was carried over into some aspects of industrial production, which still largely consisted of craftsmanship. This holistic approach was retained by the craftsmen in their handiwork; in the wisdom of the hand and the choice of raw materials in harmony with expectations of how the item would be used. This fostered a feeling for form, which has remained an important component of design training to this day.

In the 1930s, the foundations of the *folkhem* (the People´s Home)– as Swedes refer to their welfare state – were laid in a Sweden dominated by the ideas and values of the Social Democrats. One of their aspirations was to raise the quality of everyday life by improving working conditions in homes, factories and offices. Research and a rational overview became important tools.

The driving force

Housing construction was the driving force behind the achievement of greater prosperity. A good home became a citizen's right. In the area of housing research, expertise was gathered and methods developed to attain this goal. The study of the function of the home was translated into standards and the co-ordination of measurements and dimensions, ranging from the teaspoon to city planning. But the focus was always on comfort, well-being, a feeling of security – and beauty.

Strong women were behind research into everyday household things such as the can opener, the baby bonnet, and the height and width of beds. The Home Research Institute was to be industry's master. As a well-informed and alert consumer, the housewife was to steer production along better paths. Scientific studies of housework were made in order to provide convincing arguments.

The student movement of 1968 opened design students'eyes to the needs of the

Third World, of the sick and disabled, in dangerous workplaces, and to the scarcity of our natural resources. These interests found resonance in a society with strong traditions of care, caring and social responsibility, and research as a part of social development. Out of this grew a new design tradition that looked at entire processes, people in their work situations and the entire relationship between man and his tools.

In 1914, the Swedish Society for Industrial Design founded a bureau for placing artists in industry. The important thing then was to communicate to industry that technological solutions were not sufficient to make a product attractive. It was also a matter of opening their eyes to what art could be. The beautifully designed tool, utensil, machine, could also be "art," and a form of cultural expression. The artist had a new role. Technology and art need not be antagonistic. The artist's experience could provide new insights and solutions right from the beginning of the production process.

The artist was also to function as a representative user with the ability to assume roles and enter into various situations. The artist could also contribute by looking at things in different ways. "Beauty for all" was the message of the early 1900s, particularly for the home – the setting, the foundation, the frame for our lives.

Artists and architects were the first to apply an artistic eye to everyday items. At the beginning of the 1950s, designers trained as craftsmen began to adopt the rationale of functionalism and joined their talents with an expanding industry that was to give the welfare state a face. Swedish design blossomed into a material sensuality combined with an understanding of how items were used and a love of the simple and everyday. The "More Beautiful Everyday Things" had found a home in the welfare society, and were backed up by comprehensive consumer information. This also led to a deeper insight into the conditions shaping the industrial process, and the relationships between industry, market and distribution. Designs were created in collaboration with engineers, in a practical context.

Both industry and the market have since undergone major transformations. The problems are now different. But we are still convinced that the quality of everyday tasks can be raised through a close study of conditions. There is still much that can be done to improve the tools and environments that shape such a large part of our lives. It can be found in a finely tuned and harmonious interplay between man and his environment. The ideal of "More Beautiful Everyday Things" is still as valid as ever.

OPPOSITE PAGE: RESEARCHERS AT THE SWEDISH ROAD AND TRANSPORT RESEARCH INSTITUTE HAVE BEEN TESTING CAR SEATS FOR CHILDREN FOR NEARLY 30 YEARS. THIS SEAT FACES BACKWARD, AND PROVIDES THE BEST PROTECTION. NEARLY ALL SWEDISH CHILDREN RIDE SAFELY BUCKLED INTO CAR SEATS.

the
good job

BY
STEFAN FRANZÉN

PHOTO: IT IS POSSIBLE TO COMBINE A
BETTER WORK ENVIRONMENT FOR
WELDERS WITH GREATER PRODUCTIVITY
AND HIGHER QUALITY. THE INSTITUTE
OF PRODUCTION AND ENGINEERING
RESEARCH AND LINDHOLMEN
DEVELOPMENT, WITH SUPPORT FROM
THE SWEDISH WORK ENVIRONMENT FUND,
HAVE SHOWN THAT IT CAN BE DONE.

THE GOOD JOB

BY STEFAN FRANZÉN

more and more Swedish companies are realizing just how much a better work environment and better ergonomics mean to quality and productivity, and thus to competitive strength. For companies that understand that tools, machines and systems should be designed around human beings and their abilities, the future is full of opportunity. Purely technological solutions will be at a disadvantage in competition for the informed consumer of the future.

Social norms and values are constantly changing, and of course this affects working life. In the 1970s, health and safety were the most important subjects of discussions about the work environment. The strategies discussed in the 1990s are marked by a holistic approach, and the focus is increasingly on people. Companies are beginning to realize that a good work environment is not necessarily incompatible with greater efficiency and better quality.

Focus on the user

Large, complex systems are becoming increasingly common, and jobs are becoming increasingly automated. Society is only at the beginning of an explosive development of information technology, and we are facing completely new threats and opportunities in our working lives. In this new world it is imperative to know about people and how they function.

It used to be that the most important concerns of occupational health were medical and technical problems and the costs of alternative corrective measures. Today, occupational health and ergonomics generally have other implications. The emphasis has shifted to quality, productivity and ways to compete successfully on the market.

Functional design adapted to the user is already a factor in competition. In the future there will be a huge demand for the best possible interaction between people and their machines and systems.

A new attitude

With industrialism, mass production, increasingly standardized demand and increasingly fragmented jobs, there has been a shift from craftsmanship and versatility to simplification, and assembly-line work.

The early industrial organization developed jobs that were monotonous, simple, bound to machines, apparently meaningless and often directly harmful. The fight for the good job is primarily a fight against this attitude toward human beings.

Social progress has brought rising levels of education and higher living standards, and with this, people have become more independent. They are demanding more from their jobs. Most of us in the Western world have passed the stage where a job meant survival and food on the table. Today, other goals are usually more important, those which in one way or another provide satisfaction and self-realization.

Earlier efforts to improve the work environment were concentrated on production environments and factors such as noise and physical workload. The physical work environment is important, and the research of the past decades should have resulted in better workplaces and products more quickly than it has. But good jobs and good workplaces are not created simply by technical solutions to physical problems.

Progress and new knowledge have led to a focus on people's abilities and needs, not only in industry, but in other kinds of jobs as well. Work organization and psychological conditions are very important today when jobs are designed and assessed.

In Swedish companies the employers and employees often have the same notions of the qualities that are desirable. Many of the aspirations of the 1990s are backed by a common purpose.

The good job

One of the implications of the holistic view of work is that the employees' capacities are better exploited. They are allowed to use more of their professional skill and creativity. It is increasingly important that employees think and solve problems on their own, and this increases their self-esteem, motivation and flexibility.

The holistic view also reveals opportunities to expand the content of the job, increase responsibility and develop skills to handle ever higher demands. Employees have less supervision and more freedom to plan their work and define their jobs. Some companies have formed work teams that have common goals and assume responsibility not only for a part of production but also for the necessary planning and training.

With new forms for organization and work combined with new information technologies, the work teams can be in direct contact with both customers and suppliers of materials, tools and services. These are rewarding jobs for the employees, and the company becomes more flexible and efficient through having competent decision makers close to the day-to-day problems.

A competitive factor

It is not due simply to goodness of heart or government regulations that Swedish companies are increasingly interested in developing better work environments and functionally designed products. It's also because they have realized that these measures increase productivity and thus improve their competitive position.

Good tools and equipment are necessary if the employees are to do their best work and work efficiently.

ABB – a good example

As a project leader at Asea Brown Boveri, I participated in improving a bad work environment in a machine workshop. The shop had almost every conceivable type of work environment problem. Various stopgap measures had been taken to solve the acute problems that arose regularly. When the company's management decided to seriously

OPPOSITE PAGE: THE SWEDISH WORK ENVIRONMENT FUND AND THE SWEDISH TRANSPORT RESEARCH INSTITUTE SUPPORTED THE ERGONOMIC STUDIES BEHIND THE ERGO TRUCK FROM ATLET. LARS PETTERSON IS BEHIND THE DESIGN OF THE VEHICLE, WHICH WON A PRIZE FOR EXCELLENT SWEDISH DESIGN IN THE SPRING OF 1994.

tackle the problem, it provided an opportunity to do it all over from the ground up. The solutions, which were developed and introduced in collaboration with the employees, involved a new organization, new tools, new work methods and changes in product design.

The project always had the full support of management, and is a good example of a common purpose shared by a company and its employees. The result was not only a better work environment, but also more efficient production and a better product.

Market and ergonomics

New products, as well as existing products, challenge the market in various ways. Are there any special problems in marketing ergonomic design or introducing measures to improve working conditions?

The practical advantages of a good ergonomic design usually become apparent when the product is intensively used on the job, but long-term effects and values are seldom easy to demonstrate.

How can a buyer properly assess ergonomic factors and compare them with more traditional sales arguments such as price and technical specifications?

Here is where the functional design runs into a major problem. Virtually the only way to communicate feeling and understanding for the function is via experience. Only then will you be able to judge the added value the product may have. Esthetics are also

important. The design should not only be attractive, but should also give some indication of what the product is for and how it should be used.

Who is buying?

Who is it that actually has to be persuaded? The traditional purchaser is not a user. Many purchasers tend to focus on factors that are easy to compare – irrelevant technical specifications and purchase price, for example – and may neglect the really pertinent information.

This attitude, or perhaps ignorance, is of course an obstacle for the selling company, but it must not be forgotten that it also has a negative long-term effect on the purchasing company's competitive ability.

A forklift truck

To take an example: A company needs to invest in a number of new forklift trucks for a recently remodeled warehouse. A purchaser is impressed by the carrying capacity and speed of a particular model. The vehicles are to be used for light goods, however, over short distances and in cramped spaces. The performance criteria that determine the appropriateness of the vehicles are therefore quite different: maneuverability, good visibility, flexible work positions, etc. Satisfaction over the lower purchase price of the strong, speedy models did not last long.

Value for whom?

Even though the product may have considerable value to the person who is going to use it, there are other parties who for various reasons have entirely different interests. A product is always used in a context. If the new product does not fit in with existing systems of production and distribution, for example, its entry on the market will be automatically blocked.

Ergonomic innovators often try to solve too many problems at once, and may skip several steps in product development. Unfortunately, this often leads to new products that do not fit in with existing systems at all, and thus creates a virtually insurmountable marketing barrier.

There may be companies and people who do not see the problem or the product from the perspective of the user, or are not concerned about the total cost. They profit – or believe that they profit – by preserving the status quo, and therefore they block progress.

That a product or a work method is "ergonomic" is seldom a convincing argument. In order to be accepted, the new alternative must either solve a new problem or provide a better solution to an old one. Methods for long-term assessment and comparison of different investments are now being developed. Life Cycle Cost (LCC) shows the total cost and income associated with an investment from purchase to scrapping.

With this method, the future economic consequences of a bad work environment can be assessed – costs such as sick leave, occupational injury and accidents. The method often reveals that purchase price is a very small fraction of costs over the lifetime of a product.

The plasterboard

In order to make plasterboards lighter and easier to handle, it was proposed that the width should be reduced from 1200 to 900 millimeters. Even after ten years, this simple modification has still not managed to break into the systems of the producers, the distributors or the construction companies where the traditional plasterboard is handled.

In spite of the fact that it is lighter, easier to handle and more economically competitive, the narrower plasterboard has not managed to take more than a fifth of the market.

NEXT PAGE: CLEANING IS HEAVY, TIME-CONSUMING WORK. THE ELECTRIC "SVOPPER" BY ADVANCED SUPPLY REPLACES THE MOP BUCKET, AND MAKES CLEANING FIVE TIMES AS FAST. THE MACHINE IS EASY TO STEER AND CATCHES DUST RATS IN OUT-OF-THE-WAY CORNERS. ONE CHARGE IS ENOUGH FOR 1,000 SQUARE METERS.

The driving force

The reasons that ergonomic solutions seldom achieve commercial success are many and varied, but the problem must be examined from both sides: the product developer's and the market's.

The ergonomist may have several good technological solutions, but believes, perhaps all too often, that "good ergonomics" will sell itself. The market is more complicated than many realize, which has put a stop to many good ideas and products. For representatives of the market, ergonomics itself is usually irrelevant, but new and deeper knowledge of the interaction between people and machines may increase insight into what a good ergonomic solution can do for efficiency and productivity.

Ergonomists and product developers need to know more about market mechanisms, and the representatives of the market must be more receptive to the idea that ergonomic solutions can reduce a company's costs and provide a competitive advantage. A company that chooses a development strategy based on purely technological solutions, for either itself or its products, is taking a dangerous path.

The more complex and technical the world becomes, the more important knowledge about people will become. With the focus on people, technology will become an opportunity to create products and systems that are adapted to the user. Customers are becoming better informed, and are demanding more.

This analysis of future needs is in good agreement with the Swedish design tradition, which is based on The Human Dimension. It is a philosophy that never goes out of style. It is not trendy or superficial.

This is the strength of Swedish industrial design. It is combined with esthetically pleasing forms, clean and simple, without pretensions. The emphasis on user-friendliness and refined simplicity will provide a great competitive advantage in the world of the future.

OPPOSITE PAGE:
"A BETTER WORK ENVIRONMENT FOR WELDERS" HAS BEEN THE MOTTO FOR THE INSTITUTE OF PRODUCTION AND ENGINEERING RESEARCH. LINDHOLMEN DEVELOPMENT AND THE WORK ENVIRONMENT FUND. THEY GAVE TOP GRADES TO SPEEDGLAS, A WELDING FILTER OF LIGHT-SENSITIVE GLASS FROM HÖRNELL ELEKTROOPTIK AB.

recreation

BY
GUSTAF ROSELL

PHOTO: HIKING IN THE SWEDISH
WILDERNESS REQUIRES TOUGH,
COMFORTABLE CLOTHING AND SHOES.
KLÄTTERMUSEN OUTDOOR WEAR IS
DESIGNED BY LALLA ERSARE. THE HIKING
SHOES ARE FROM LUNDHAGS.

BY GUSTAF ROSELL

Swedish products for sports and outdoor activities reflect the unique character of the Swedish wilderness. Being in the mountains, on skis in the winter or on foot in the summer, is one of the most popular ways to spend a vacation. The central role of working life is diminishing. The value changes have already led to new attitudes to leisure time. Adventures and challenges are more important to people than things. Their leisure time is supposed to offer more than amusement.

Outdoor life in Sweden gets its unique character largely from the Swedish *allemansrätt*, which guarantees the right for all to enjoy the forests and mountains, and to pick berries, mushrooms and wildflowers, so long as they do not damage crops or disturb the landowner.

Much of today's leisure clothing owes its design to equipment developed for working life. Professional fishermen, sailors, hunters and lumberjacks need to have durable and comfortable clothes. Their equipment has provided models for leisure wear at sea and in the wilderness.

In Sweden, knowledge of functional clothing has been developed in a close cooperation between the potential users and researchers, designers and companies which are interested in producing new products. The function is always in focus.

During the past decade the images of sports clothes and work clothes have become more and more alike.

The big commercial interests in professional sports have accelerated development of new materials and equipment in order to reach new heights and set new records. This knowledge has gradually been applied to sports goods for private usage.

In Sweden safety and freedom have been important objectives in consumer policy. Such thinking can be illustrated in products such as bike helmets and child seats for bikes and cars, designed to avoid or reduce injuries in case of an accident.

Many manufacturers of outdoor products are small, typical entrepreneurial companies. Although a formally trained designer is seldom involved in the design, these products are alike in a special way. Form, with few compromises, is governed by function. A fairly common characteristic is a certain traditionalism that contrasts with the high-technology materials and design. Mass-produced items reflect an artisanal heritage. Delicate parts are often made by hand, which gives the products a special expression. The outdoor activities in Sweden are determined by the seasons.

Autumn

Autumn is above all the season for hunting – particularly elk hunting. Elk hunting has an appealing egalitarian aura for Swedes. Company managers and truck drivers may belong to the same hunting teams. This has so far been possible because the rent of hunting rights has been kept low even though demand for hunting territory is considerable. The supply of game is also very good, especially elk. The hunting equipment is remarkable for its traditionalism. No changes are made unless there are compelling functional reasons.

Winter

With Sweden's climate, winter sports are obviously important. In addition to alpine skiing, Swedes go on cross-country ski tours like the Norwegians and Finns do. The Swedish mountains have plenty of winter trails. Some of them are quite challenging, while others are more leisurely and have rest cabins at convenient intervals.

Equipment can be either traditional or high-tech. Perhaps the most interesting products are those in which the two have been successfully combined – clothing and boots, for example. Other common sports are ice fishing and long-distance ice skating.

Spring

Many winter sports are actually springtime activities, as there is still plenty of snow in northern Sweden. Fishing also begins in the spring. In April, for example, there is salmon fishing in rivers and streams. Fishing equipment made in Sweden is mostly for fly fishing, rod fishing and deep-sea fishing.

Playgrounds have been given considerable emphasis and pedagogic attention for more than 20 years. When the large high-rise apartments were constructed in the 1960s it was considered extremely important that the children could nevertheless play outdoors.

Summer

Sweden is surrounded by water and has several archipelagos, both along the east coast in the Baltic and along the west coast, facing the North Sea. On both coasts boating, and especially sailing, is a very popular way to spend a vacation. Sailing in the Swedish archipelago is different from sailing on the Continent. Nights are often spent in natural coves on one of the many islands. There are 25,000 islands in the Stockholm archipelago alone.

The most beautiful boats are those that have been designed to sail as fast as possible in the relatively sheltered waters of the archipelago. These island cruisers are long, slim yachts with plenty of sail, and preferably built of wood.

Summer is also when many people take to the wilderness. Wilderness hikers often live in tents rather than in the cabins that most of them use in the winter. More exotic sports that are gaining in popularity are whitewater boating and mountain climbing.

Many people spend their summer vacations in their little red cabins – one of the most Swedish of phenomena. The cabins are all over the country, and many of them are beautifully situated near lakes and rivers, or on islands in the archipelago. The color, called Falu red, has been manufactured at the copper mine in Falun since 1616. It has been common in the Swedish countryside for well over a century, and has become something of a national symbol.

OPPOSITE PAGE:
SAFETELY ABOARD IN CALM OR STORM. GLP ENTERPRISE DEVELOPED THIS STRONG, LIGHTWEIGHT SAFETY HARNESS IN COLLABORATION WITH EXPERIENCED SAILORS.

AUTHORS

MARIA BENKTZON,
PROFESSOR AND INDUSTRIAL DESIGNER,
ERGONOMI DESIGN GRUPPEN, STOCKHOLM.

OLLE BOBJER,
ERGONOMIST,
ERGONOMI DESIGN GRUPPEN, STOCKHOLM.

TORSTEN DAHLIN,
PROFESSOR IN INDUSTRIAL ERGONOMY,
SWEDISH INDUSTRIAL DESIGN FOUNDATION, STOCKHOLM.

STEFAN FRANZÉN,
PROJECT MANAGER,
SWEDISH WORK ENVIRONMENT FUND, STOCKHOLM.

ROLAND KADEFORS,
PROFESSOR IN APPLIED PHYSIOLOGY,
LINDHOLMEN DEVELOPMENT, GÖTEBORG.

ÅSA KILBOM,
PROFESSOR IN APPLIED WORK PHYSIOLOGY,
NATIONAL INSTITUTE OF OCCUPATIONAL HEALTH, STOCKHOLM.

GUNILLA LUNDAHL,
JOURNALIST,
STOCKHOLM.

ULF MANNERVIK
ECONOMIST,
CHALMERS UNIVERSITY OF TECHNOLOGY, GÖTEBORG.

DANIELE MASCANZONI,
ATTACHÉ OF SCIENCE AND TECHNOLOGY,
CONSULATE GENERAL OF SWEDEN, MILAN.

ANTY PANSERA,
CRITIC AND HISTORIAN OF THE INDUSTRIAL DESIGN,
MILAN.

GUSTAF ROSELL,
PRODUCT DESIGNER,
LILJEFORS & ROSELL, STOCKHOLM.

LENA SPERLING,
PROFESSOR IN CONSUMER TECHNOLOGY,
LINDHOLMEN DEVELOPMENT, GÖTEBORG.

KERSTIN WICKMAN,
DESIGN EDITOR
FORM, STOCKHOLM.